Introducing Religions

Hinduism

Sue Penney

www.heinemann.co.uk/library
Visit our website to find out more information about Heinemann Library books.

To order:
☎ Phone 44 (0) 1865 888066
🖹 Send a fax to 44 (0) 1865 314091
🖥 Visit the Heinemann Bookshop at www.heinemann.co.uk/library to browse our catalogue and order online.

First published in Great Britain by Heinemann Library, Halley Court, Jordan Hill, Oxford OX2 8EJ, part of Harcourt Education.
Heinemann is a registered trademark of Harcourt Education Ltd.

Editorial: Clare Lewis
Design: Jo Hinton-Malivoire and Q2A Creative
Illustrations: Gecko Limited
Picture Research: Erica Newbury
Production: Helen McCreath

Printed and bound in China by WKT.

10 digit ISBN 0 431 06657 4
13 digit ISBN 978 0 431 06657 8
10 09 08 07 06
10 9 8 7 6 5 4 3 2 1

British Library Cataloguing in Publication Data
Penney, Sue
Hinduism (Introducing Religions – 2nd edition)
294.5
A full catalogue record for this book is available from the British Library.

Acknowledgements
The publishers would like to thank the following for permission to reproduce photographs:
The Ancient Art and Architecture Collection p. 10; Mohamed Ansar/Impact Photos pp. 34, 45; Andes Press Agency p. 24; The Bridgeman Art Library p. 14; The J Allan Cash Photo Library p. 29; Circa Photo Library pp. 19, 24, 31, 38, 42 (left); Comstock p. 28; Douglas Dickins pp. 17, 22; C M Dixon p. 20; Ben Edwards/Impact Photos p. 43; Getty Images/Lonely Planet Images p. 18; Sally and Richard Greenhill p. 46 (below), 47; Sunil Gupta/Network p. 35; Ian Happs pp. 12, 21; Judy Harrison/Format Partners p. 36; The Hutchison Library pp. 30, 44, 49; Roshini Kempadoo/Format Partners p. 42 (right); Christine Osborne Pictures p. 8; Ann and Bury Peerless pp. 11, 13, 15, 16, 32, 33, 48; Sarita Sharma/Format Partners p. 46 (top); Topham Picturepoint pp. 23, 27, 37, 40, 41.

The photograph on the previous page is reproduced by permission of Corbis/Chris Hellier.

Cover photograph of a young Hindu holy man dressed as Lord Shiva, reproduced with permission of Corbis/Amit Bhargava.

The publishers would like to thank Yogesh Patel for his assistance in the preparation of this book.

Every effort has been made to contact copyright holders of any material reproduced in this book. Any omissions will be rectified in subsequent printings if notice is given to the publishers.

The paper used to print this book comes from sustainable resources.

Contents

Words that are printed in bold, **like this**, are explained in the glossary on page 50.

MAP: where the main religions began

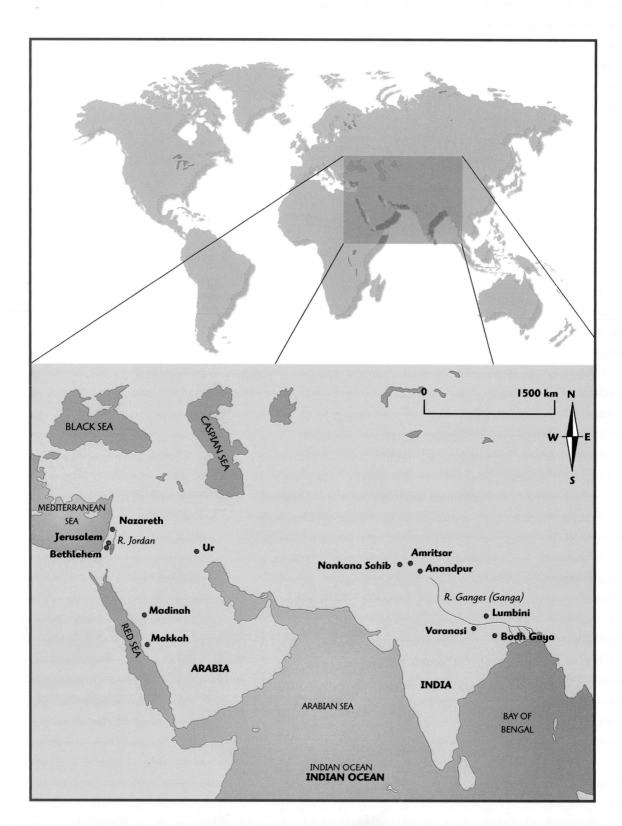

TIMECHART: when the main religions began

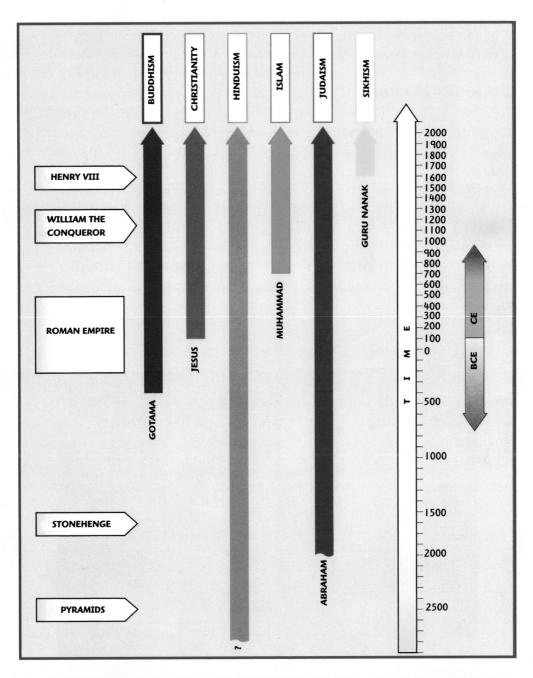

Note about dating systems *In this book dates are not called* BC *and* AD, *which is the Christian dating system. The letters* BCE *and* CE *are used instead.* BCE *stands for "Before the Common Era" and* CE *stands for "Common Era".* BCE *and* CE *can be used by people of all religions, Christians too. The year numbers are not changed.*

Introducing Hinduism

This section tells you something about what Hindus believe.

When did Hinduism begin?

Hinduism is the oldest of the world's religions. It began so long ago that no one really knows when, but it was at least 5,000 years ago. It began in the northern part of India.

Over the years, it has formed lots of different branches. Different Hindus may believe quite different things, even though they all follow the religion of Hinduism.

Sanatan dharma

Most Hindus do not talk about their religion as Hinduism. They call it **Sanatan dharma**. This means "**eternal** truth". Eternal means something that lasts for ever. In other words, Hindus believe that their religion teaches things which have always been true and always will be.

The truths are written about in the Hindu **holy** books. The books are called the **Vedas** (see page 14). Most Hindus believe that the Vedas contain the most important part of their beliefs.

What do Hindus believe?

Hindus believe that there is one Great Power. Some Hindus would call it God.

Hindu children worshipping at home

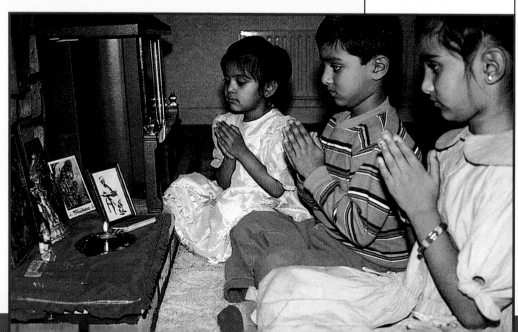

The Hindu name is **Brahman**. Most Hindus say that this power can be seen through gods and goddesses.

Hindus believe that everything has a **soul**. Your soul is your spirit, which lives on after your body has died.

Hindus believe that when you die, your soul moves on to live in another person, or an animal or plant. Where it goes depends on how you have lived your life. Hindus aim to become good enough to stop this rebirth happening, so the soul can join with Brahman.

This is the sign which means **Aum**.

Brahman

Hindus believe that Brahman is everywhere, and everything is what it is because Brahman is in it. This is a complicated idea, but Hindus explain it like this.

Think of water which has salt in it. You cannot see the salt, and you may not know it is there unless you taste the water. Yet even the smallest drop of this water has some salt in it, and all of the water is what it is because of the salt.

Hindus say that in the same way, Brahman is in everything that is in the universe, and Brahman makes everything what it is.

Hindu gods

This section tells you about the gods who are most important in Hinduism.

There are three gods who are most important in Hinduism. Many Hindus **worship** them.

These three gods are called Brahma, who **creates** things, Vishnu, who **preserves** things, and Shiva, who destroys things. Hindus believe that these three gods work together in a pattern which never ends. Everything is made, lasts for a time, and is then destroyed.

Hindus do not often worship Brahma today, so this section is about Vishnu and Shiva.

Vishnu

Vishnu is worshipped with several different names. This is because Hindus believe that he has come to earth many times. Each time, the earth was in danger. He came to protect it. The two most important times were when he came as the god Rama, and when he came as the god Krishna.

The story of the god Rama is in a long poem called the *Ramayana* (see page 17). Krishna's story is part of the poem called the *Mahabharata* (see page 16).

Krishna is worshipped by more Hindus than any other god.

An old carving showing Vishnu, Brahma, and Shiva

Shiva is also called Lord of the Dance.

Shiva

Shiva is worshipped by about a quarter of all Hindus. He is in charge of destruction. He is frightening because of his power, but Hindus also believe that he is kind. He destroys things that are old or no longer needed, but it is only because they are destroyed that new things can happen.

His four hands show that he holds the power of life and death and good and evil.

Hindu gods and goddesses

There are hundreds of gods and goddesses in Hinduism. At first, most people probably thought these gods and goddesses were real, like people. Some people still do. Most Hindus today think they are a way of describing **Brahman**, the Great Power.

Human beings cannot fully understand what Brahman is. Hindus believe that if they worship a god they can understand, this will help them to worship Brahman properly, even though they do not fully understand what Brahman is.

Gods and goddesses

This section tells you about some popular gods and goddesses.

There are hundreds and hundreds of gods and goddesses in Hinduism, and a Hindu can choose to **worship** any one or more of them.

Hindus usually choose one that their family worships, or one that they feel has helped them in some way. Hindus do not believe that any one god or particular way of worship is better or worse than any other.

Shakti

Many of the gods are described as having "families". Shakti is Shiva's wife. She is sometimes called the Mother Goddess. Like many gods and goddesses, she is sometimes fierce, sometimes kind. She has more then one name to show these different sides of her character. In her fierce form, she is Kali. Kali is very frightening. Shakti's kind and gentle side is called Parvati.

The goddess Kali.

Lakshmi

Lakshmi is the wife of Vishnu. She is the goddess of beauty and good fortune.

Ganesha

Ganesha has an elephant's head. The stories say that he is Shiva's son. Shiva cut off Ganesha's head by mistake when he was in a temper. He gave him an elephant's head in its place. Many Hindus believe Ganesha can help solve problems.

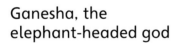
Ganesha, the elephant-headed god

Belief is like a mountain

Hinduism allows many different ways of worship, and different gods to worship. Hindus say that what is important is that everyone – Hindu or not – should worship God in the way that is right for them.

An old Indian teaching says that religion is like a mountain. There may be many paths that go to the top. Some of them are harder to climb than others, but different people have different abilities. The important thing is that you get to the top. Once you get to the top, it does not matter how you got there.

Holy books

This section tells you about the holy books which are most important for Hindus.

Hinduism began thousands of years ago. In that time, many **holy** books have been written.

Some praise the gods, some tell people how to **worship**, some are about Hindu beliefs.

Most of the books were written in **Sanskrit**, one of the oldest languages in the world.

Today, Sanskrit is used only in the religion. People do not use it for speaking or writing.

The Vedas

The **Vedas** are the oldest of the Hindu holy books. They contain the basic truths which Hindus believe do not change. They were written down in about 1200 BCE, but date back to about 3,000 years before that.

The teachings were passed on by **Gurus** to their students. In those days, not many people could read and write, and people had to learn things off by heart. It was the best way to remember them.

The most important Veda is the first. This is the Rig Veda. It contains over 1,000 poems.

The writing on this page is in Sanskrit.

Reading the holy books

The Upanishads

The Upanishads are the last part of each Veda. The name comes from Sanskrit words which mean "sit down near". People used to sit down near wise men who were teaching about the Vedas, and learn from them.

The Laws of Manu

Manu was a wise teacher whose teachings were written down in about 300 CE.

The Laws of Manu tell Hindus about how they should live. They also contain instructions for **priests**.

What is a seed?

A father was teaching his son about religion. He told his son to fetch a fruit from a nearby tree. Then he told him to break open the fruit and find the seeds. The son did so. Then the father told him to break open a seed. The son did so. The father asked what was inside the seed. The son said there was nothing there. The father agreed. Then he pointed out that the huge tree had grown from a tiny seed just like this one.

   The lesson of the story was that just as you cannot see the important part of the seed, so you cannot see **Brahman**, the spirit which is in everything.

(*From the Chandogya Upanishad*)

Holy poems

This section tells you about two important Hindu poems.

There are two very long poems which are part of the Hindu **holy** books. One is called the *Mahabharata*. The other is called the *Ramayana*. The poems teach important lessons about the Hindu religion.

Many Hindu actors and dancers use parts of the stories of these poems in their acts.

The *Mahabharata*

The *Mahabharata* is the longest poem in the world. It has 100,000 verses. It was written by many different people over hundreds of years.

The main story is about a quarrel between two royal families. One family tricks the other and there is a great battle. For many Hindus, the most important part of the poem is the part that is called the *Bhagavad Gita*.

In the *Bhagavad Gita*, the god Krishna teaches a prince of one of the families about his duty, and the right way to live and worship.

This painting shows a scene from the Bhagavad Gita.

A dance showing part of the Ramayana

The *Ramayana*

The *Ramayana* is not as long as the *Mahabharata*, but it still contains 24,000 verses. It was probably written down in about 100 CE and is much older than the *Mahabharata*.

It tells the story of Prince Rama and his wife Sita. Sita is kidnapped by a wicked monster called Ravana.

Helped by the monkey god Hanuman and his monkey army, Rama finds Sita and rescues her. Ravana is killed and everything ends happily.

Hindu dance

Dancing is very important in Hinduism. The stories say that it was a gift from the gods. Hindus believe that through watching the dances, they can learn more about the gods and the things that happened to them. The dancing takes many years to learn, because there are many rules. Masks and costumes show who are the heroes and who are the villains. Movements of the hands help the story to be told without any words.

Half moon   Peacock   Greeting

17

Worship in the home

This section tells you about how Hindus worship at home.

Hindus believe that their religion affects everything they do. They believe that God is in everything, so everything in their life can be counted as **worship**.

Cooking a meal or sweeping the floor can be worship if it is done properly and with care. The most common form of special worship is called **puja**.

Puja

Puja means making offerings to an **image** or picture of one of the gods or goddesses. Images and pictures are to help people worship. They are ways of showing **Brahman**.

A Hindu house always has a **shrine**. This may be quite small and simple – perhaps a shelf on a wall. If the family can afford it, a shrine may take up a whole room. The shrine always has an image or picture of one or more of the gods or goddesses surrounded by flowers and perfume.

Hindus worship at least once a day. The point of worship is to spend time with God, so Hindus prepare for it very carefully. An **image** is washed. Small gifts are offered – a flower petal or a grain of rice is enough.

While they are making puja, Hindus repeat verses from the **holy** books. They begin with the word **Aum**, which Hindus believe is a way of describing Brahman.

A puja ceremony

A Hindu boy praying at a shrine

They may also **meditate**. Meditation means emptying your mind of other thoughts, so that you think only about God. Worshippers sometimes put their hands together, and touch their forehead. They do not wear shoes, and they stand, or sit with their legs crossed.

They may kneel and touch the ground in front of the image with their forehead. These are all ways of showing respect.

In a shrine

To show respect to the image, the shrine is surrounded by flowers and perfume. The perfume often comes from sticks of **incense**, which are burned and give off a sweet smell.

There may also be a special bottle made of copper which contains water from the River Ganga. This river is in India and is also called the Ganges. It is a **holy** river for Hindus. Images in a shrine are often coloured blue. Blue is considered a special colour because Krishna is usually shown as blue. This is to show that he is holy.

Worship in a temple

This section tells you about how Hindus worship in temples.

A **temple** is a place that is specially for **worship**. Hindus worship at home, too, but temple worship is special. Many Hindu temples in India are small and simple.

Other temples are large and beautifully decorated with wooden and stone carvings. Some temples can be like small villages themselves. The proper name for a temple is a **mandir**.

Even very small temples have at least one **priest**. His job is to look after the **image** or images of the god. All temples have a **shrine** room where the image is kept, and a room where the priest lives.

There is always a river or other water so that people can wash before they worship. This is a special washing to make them fit for worship. It has nothing to do with being dirty.

Worship in a temple

Worship begins before dawn, when the image of the god or goddess is "woken up" by the priest. He says prayers, beginning with the word **Aum**. Then the image is bathed and dried. It has special paste put on it, and may have flowers hung round it.

In a large temple, the image will have been in a sleeping room overnight, so it will be taken back to the shrine room. Then offerings will be made to it. Worship may take place several times a day.

A large temple in India

Group worship

Hindus often worship alone. Sometimes, though, a priest may say prayers in front of a group of people. When this happens, the worship is usually in three parts. In the first part, people sing poems from the **Vedas**. In the second part, they light a small fire and say prayers. In the third part, a small tray with five lights on it is waved in front of the image. The people hold their hands over the flames, then wipe them over their head. They believe that this gives them blessings from God.

This boy is wearing tilak.

At the temple, people take off their shoes to show respect.

They give the gifts they have brought to the priest, who takes them into the shrine room. Ordinary people do not go into the shrine room except when there is a **festival**. The gifts are usually small, perhaps some fruit or flowers.

During worship, people put a dot or stripes of special powder on their foreheads. This is called **tilak**. It shows that the person has been to worship, and the shape shows which god they have worshipped.

Pilgrimage

This section tells you about some of the special places where Hindus go on pilgrimage.

A **pilgrimage** is a special journey which people make because of their religion. Many Hindus feel that going on a journey like this is an important part of their **worship**.

Why do people go on pilgrimage?

Most people go on a pilgrimage because they want to visit a special place. Often this is a place where the god they worship appeared to people, or has an important **temple**. Sometimes they want to pray for something special, and they believe their prayer is more likely to be answered if they are in a **holy** place.

Where do people go?

There are hundreds of places of pilgrimage all over India. Some may be only a day's journey, but many pilgrims take weeks or even months to walk to their chosen place.

They may save up for most of their life to be able to make the journey. They believe that difficulties make the pilgrimage more worthwhile.

When they get to the temple or **shrine**, most pilgrims lie or sit on the floor in front of the sacred **images**. They may also walk around the shrines in a clockwise direction to show that God is the centre of their lives.

The Temple of Jaganath in India

Worshippers bathing in the River Ganga at Varanasi

Varanasi

Varanasi is the most holy city in India. It is sometimes called Benares. It is on the banks of the River Ganga (Ganges), which is a holy river.

There are special platforms called **ghats** beside the river where people can go to bathe and offer **puja**. Bathing in the river is important, because Hindus believe that it pleases God to do so.

The ghats are also where dead bodies are **cremated**. The ashes are thrown on the river.

Main places of pilgrimage

Apart from Varanasi, there are four other important places of pilgrimage in India. They are at the four corners of the country. Jaganath Puri is on the east coast, Badrinath is in the north, Dwarka is in the west. These three are temples to Vishnu. Rameshwaram in the south is a temple to Shiva. Many pilgrims try to visit the temples sometime in their life.

At Jaganath Puri the image of Jaganath (another name for Vishnu) is put on a huge cart to be pulled through the streets. The cart is so big that it has given us the word juggernaut, for a big lorry.

Hindu belief

This section tells you a little about the most important Hindu beliefs.

Dharma
Dharma means duty. Duty is something which you should do, but which no one makes you do.

Dharma depends on your family, your job and many other things. It includes **worshipping** God, not hurting other people or animals, being honest, and doing your job as well as you possibly can.

Hindus believe that doing dharma well is important.

Doing a job well is part of dharma.

Reincarnation
Reincarnation is the belief that your **soul** moves on to another being when you die. Hindus call the soul the **atman**. They believe that the atman in everything is the same. So, there is no difference in the atman of a plant or animal and a human being.

Hindus believe that the atman moves in a series of steps. It begins in plants and animals, and moves up to human beings. Whether you live a good or bad life decides what happens to your atman when you die.

Karma

Karma means action. It is the way Hindus explain how the atman moves from one being to another. A good karma in this life will mean a good life next time. A bad karma in this life will mean a hard life next time.

Hindus do not believe that you will be judged by God at the end of your life. The way you live decides whether your next life will be the same, or a step up or down. Some Hindus believe that a step can be missed if you have been very good or very bad.

Reincarnation of the atman

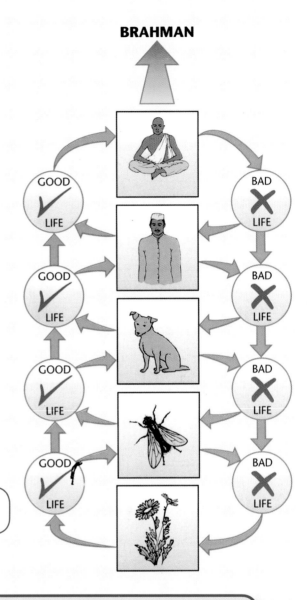

BRAHMAN

What happens in the end?

Every Hindu hopes to be able to break out of the cycle of dying and being born again. When this happens, the atman can go back to **Brahman**, which is where it came from and where it belongs.

Hindus describe this by saying that it is like a river flowing into the sea. This can only happen when a soul becomes completely pure, and is not affected by anything which happens on earth.

You will understand this better when you have read the section on yogas on pages 26–27.

The four paths to Brahman

This section tells you about the different ways in which Hindus work to break out of the cycle of birth and death.

Hindus believe there are four ways in which a person can live so that their **soul** can escape from the birth–rebirth cycle. The four ways are often called paths. Anybody can use any of the paths, and people often follow different paths at different times in their life.

The path of knowledge
This means knowing about the religion. Hindus who follow this path need a very good teacher, and they must study the religion very carefully. They follow a pattern for their life.

The path of meditation
Meditation means concentrating so hard that you forget everything around you. You can only follow this path if your mind is free of things like work, home, or family that might worry you.

Young Hindus in Britain learning about their religion

Meditation

The path of love
This path means choosing a particular god or goddess and making sure that you spend all your life **worshipping** them. Hindus following this path pray and make **puja** to the god or goddess. They also go on **pilgrimages** to worship them. The god or goddess they worship is the most important thing in their life.

The path of doing your best
Many Hindus think that for ordinary people this is the best path. It means doing your dharma – your duty – as well as you possibly can. Dharma is different for everyone, so each person has to decide for themselves what this path means for them and then work hard to follow it.

Yoga
The Hindu name for the four paths which Hindus follow are the yogas.

Many people in Western countries think that yoga means special exercises and breathing to clear your mind. This is part of yoga, but it really comes from the path of meditation which Hindus call Raja-Yoga.

The Upanishads give advice about what you should do to prepare to meditate. They say that you should find somewhere clean and quiet which is sheltered from the wind. It should not have any rubbish or anything ugly. It should be beautiful and have the sound of running water. These things can help you concentrate.

The four stages of life

This section tells you about the way Hindus often live their lives.

Hinduism teaches that there are four stages of life. They are called the four **ashramas**.

The student
From about age 8 to 20, young people should start to learn about Hinduism.

The householder
The second stage is the **grihastha**, the householder. Householders are expected to work for their living, and marry and have a family.

The forest dweller
When the family are grown up and the person is getting older – some people say about 50 years old – they should leave their home and friends. They should go to live on their own, in a place where they can be quiet. This third stage is to learn to give up everything that they enjoy. They should concentrate only on their religion. It is a time to prepare for leaving the body behind when they die.

The holy man
The **sannyasin** is the last stage. It is usually only taken by men. Sannyasin is the Hindu word for a **holy** man. It is quite common in India to see holy men walking through the streets or sitting by the side of the road teaching.

A sannyasin has no home. He usually has only the clothes he wears and a bowl in which to put food that he has been given.

A sannyasin

In India, cows are allowed to wander where they like.

He has given up all responsibilities, and can spend all his time thinking about his religion. (You may understand this more easily if you look back at page 25.)

Of course, not all Hindus live like this. Many do not want to give up their home and family when they get older. They stay in the second stage until the end of their life.

Respecting all living things

Hindus believe that the atman, the soul which is in everything, is the same, so they respect everything that is alive. Many Hindus do not eat meat. Even if they do eat meat, no Hindu will eat any meat from a cow.

For Hindus, the cow is holy. Some people think this is because the white cow stands for the **atman**. Cows are milked and cow dung is used for fuel, but the animal itself is never hurt. In many parts of India, cows are protected, and wander where they like, even in towns and cities.

Divali

This section tells you about the Hindu festival of Divali.

India is an enormous country, and many **festivals** are not celebrated in the same way in different parts of the country.

Hindus in other countries of the world may celebrate them in a different way again. The same festival may remember quite different stories, depending on where it is being celebrated.

For almost all Hindus, Divali is the most important festival of the year.

Divali

Divali takes place at the end of the Hindu month of Ashwin, so it is in October or November of the Western calendar. In some places it lasts for three days, but it is more usual for it to last for five days.

Divali means lights, and Hindus decorate their homes, **temples**, and other important buildings with rows of lights. Years ago, small lamps made of clay were used. They were called divas, and this gives the festival its name.

Lighting candles for Divali

Celebrating Divali at a temple in Britain

Divali remembers several different stories. One of the most popular stories comes from the *Ramayana* (see page 17). It tells how Prince Rama won the battle against the wicked demon Ravana, and found his wife Sita. They returned home, and Rama became king. Lamps were lit all over the city to welcome Rama home.

Other popular stories are about how the god Vishnu won a battle against a wicked giant, and how he tricked a king named Bali.

How Divali is celebrated
Divali is a festival which people celebrate with their families. They give each other presents and share meals with friends and relations. Sending cards is becoming more popular, especially with Hindus who live in Western countries.

There are bonfires and fireworks, and singing and dancing. The idea is to show that darkness can be driven away by light. This shows that in the same way evil can be driven away by good.

Other festivals (1)

This section tells you about three Hindu festivals.

Janmashtami
Janmashtami celebrates the birthday of the god Krishna. **Temples** are specially decorated, and so are **shrines** which have an image of the god Krishna. In the stories about Krishna, he was born at midnight, so many Hindus will spend all night in the temple.

At midnight, there is singing and dancing, before everyone shares specially made sweets. The most important story about Krishna is the Bhagavad Gita. Many temples organize special non-stop readings to celebrate the **festival**. They go on for eight days and nights, and are timed so that they finish at midnight on Krishna's birthday.

Navaratri
Navaratri means "nine-nights", and this is the length of the festival. Most of the celebrations of Navaratri are to celebrate Shakti, the mother goddess (see page 12). She has many different names. For Navaratri she is Durga, a soldier who rides on a lion.

Durga is very fierce, but Hindus also believe she cares about people, especially mothers. So Navaratri is an important festival for families.

A statue of baby Krishna in a temple

Dassehra

Dassehra and Navaratri are sometimes called the same festival, because Dassehra is the first night after the end of Navaratri.

At Dassehra, an image of the goddess Durga is taken to the nearest river and washed. Hindus believe all their bad luck disappears into the river, too.

Dassehra is also a time when Hindus remember the battle that Rama had with the demon Ravana. There are bonfires, and statues of Ravana are burned.

The story of Dassehra reminds people that good should overcome evil. It is a time when Hindus try to make up any quarrels which they have had in the past year.

This huge statue of Ravana is ready to be burned.

The god Krishna

The god Krishna is the eighth appearance on earth of the god Vishnu. There are many stories about his life. When he was young, he used to play naughty tricks on people. His special friend was a milkmaid called Radha.

Once, Krishna saved a village from a huge snake which was threatening the villagers. When he grew up, he saved a kingdom from a cruel king. He taught the prince in the Bhagavad Gita. Hindus believe that these stories teach lessons. They show how much people should care about each other.

Other festivals (2)

This section tells you about some other Hindu festivals.

Holi

Holi is a spring **festival**. It gets its name from Holika, a cruel princess who tried to kill a boy who **worshipped** Vishnu. He did not die because he kept repeating the names of God. This reminds Hindus how important it is to trust God.

Many Hindus remember stories about when Krishna was young and used to play tricks on people. Holi is a time for practical jokes. It is a festival full of fun.

Raksha Bandhan

Raksha Bandhan takes place in July or August (Shravan in the Indian calendar).

At Raksha Bandhan, a girl ties a silk or cotton bracelet around her brother's wrist. She hopes that it will protect him from danger. It is also a sign that he will protect her. This comes from a story about the god Indra. His wife had tied a magic string around his wrist and it saved him from an evil demon.

Ramnavami

Ramnavami is the birthday of the god Rama. It takes place in March or April (Vaishakha in the Indian calendar).

Raksha Bandhan

Drawing special patterns is part of celebrating New Year.

Rama is a very popular god, and many Hindus worship him. In the **temple**, there are readings from the *Ramayana*. People sing the Ramanama, which is a list of all the names of Rama. Many Hindus **fast** at Ramnavami.

New Year

Hindus may celebrate New Year at different times, depending on where they live or where their families came from. New Year is always a chance for Hindus to turn over a new leaf, and make changes in their life. Houses are cleaned or painted. Everyone wears new or clean clothes.

Fasting

Many Hindu festivals are days of **fasting**. In some religions, fasting means not eating anything at all.

Fasting for Hindus means not eating certain foods. For example, foods like meat, fish, onions, rice, or wheat. However, on fast days things like fresh fruit and milk are allowed. So is ghee, which is butter which has been heated so that it is a clear liquid. It is often used for cooking.

These are the sorts of foods which many families in India who are very poor would not normally eat. Eating them on fast days during a festival is a way of making the festival more special.

Hindu history

This section tells you something about the history of Hinduism.

The beginnings of Hinduism
No one knows exactly when Hinduism began, but it was about 5,000 years ago. It started among people who lived in the north of the country we call India. They **worshipped** gods of fire, water, and wind.

Then the country was taken over by people from the country we call Iran. They worshipped gods of the sun, moon, and stars. As the years passed, these two sorts of worship joined together.

Gradually, people began to believe that the different gods were really all ways of looking at **Brahman**, the Great Power.

Hinduism and Buddhism
Buddhists follow the teachings of Gotama, the Buddha. He lived in India in the fifth century BCE. Many people who had been Hindus began to follow the teachings of the Buddha. By the third century BCE, almost everyone in India was **Buddhist**.

Hindu teachers saw that to survive, Hinduism needed to be more organized. They began writing down books like the **Vedas** and the great poems. They spent a lot of time teaching, and the lessons of the stories became clearer.

Hinduism and Islam
After about 1100 CE, **Muslims** ruled India for about 300 years. Muslims did not like the way Hindus worshipped, and many Hindu temples were pulled down. Hinduism became less popular.

Hindus worshipping today

When India was divided

The British stopped ruling India in 1947. India became independent and became a Hindu country. The new country of Pakistan was made, to be a Muslim country. This caused a lot of problems.

Many Hindus who were living in the part that became Pakistan moved to India. Many Muslims who were living in India moved to Pakistan. This meant that thousands of people had to move to new areas. They had to leave their homes and their jobs.

It was a very difficult time. There were riots in many towns and cities, and thousands of people were killed.

In the 19th century, the rulers of India were the British. They ruled at a time when the world was changing very quickly. Hinduism had to show that it was still important in the changing world. Many famous Hindu teachers worked hard to show that Hinduism was a world religion.

Today, most people living in India are Hindu.

Hinduism is a mixture of many beliefs. It accepts many different views. Hindus say that all religions are a search for truth.

A crowded train taking Muslims to Pakistan in 1947

The caste system

This section tells you about different groups of people in India.

Different people are good at different things. Hinduism teaches that this is mainly because of their previous lives.

The teaching about dharma (duty) tells Hindus that it is important that they make the most of their abilities. From this came the idea that some groups of people were good at particular things. For hundreds of years, Hindus have been divided into groups. These groups are called **varnas**.

The four varnas

There are four groups or varnas. The most important group are **Brahmins**. They are **priests**. The second group are **Kshatriyas**. They are soldiers. The third group are **Vaishyas**. They are shopkeepers and farmers. The fourth group are **Shudras**. They are servants for the other three groups. Below these four groups are the **Harijans**, the untouchables.

These four main groups then divided into many smaller groups. The smaller groups are called **jatis** or **castes**. Your jati depends on the jati of your family. Some jatis are "higher" or "lower" than other jatis.

A Hindu priest, who is a Brahmin

People used to be very strict about not having anything to do with people who came from a lower jati than their own. For example, people would only marry someone from the same jati, and they would not eat food prepared by someone from a lower jati. Some people are still very strict about this. This way of dividing people into groups is called the caste system. It is the way that people in India have lived for hundreds of years.

In the last 50 years, things have changed. People do jobs outside their varna. People who live in cities cannot be so careful about who they meet or talk to. It is more difficult to keep the rules about jatis so strictly. But most people still know what jati they belong to, and what this means to other people.

In many villages in India, the caste laws are still strictly kept even though it is now against the law to treat people differently because of their caste.

Harijans

The lowest group in India are the Harijans. They are below the four varnas, and do the dirtiest jobs. For many years, no other Hindu would have anything to do with anyone from this group. They were called untouchables, and they were not allowed in temples or public places.

The Hindu leader Gandhi (see pages 40–41) tried to improve the lives of untouchables. He gave them the name Harijans, which means "children of God". Since 1947 it has been against the law in India to call people untouchable or to treat them differently from anyone else. Today, there are about 100 million people in this group in India.

Mahatma Gandhi

This section tells you about an important Hindu.

Gandhi's early life
Mohandas Karamchand Gandhi was born in 1869 in a small town in India. He was a shy, quiet child. When Gandhi was 16, his father died. The family had very little money.

Gandhi needed to earn his living. One of his friends suggested that he should go to England and study law.

Gandhi in South Africa
Gandhi returned to India after he had passed his exams in 1891. He found it hard to get a job, and he was offered work in South Africa.

While he was in South Africa, he realized that black people were being treated unfairly. He decided to try to improve the way they were treated. He became a fighter for freedom.

He did not fight in the same way as other people. He said that using violence to get what you want is wrong. He talked about **ahimsa** – non-violent fighting. He said that you should stand up for what you believe without using violence.

Gandhi's work in India
Gandhi went back to India in 1915. For the rest of his life, he worked to improve the lives of the untouchables (see page 39). He was very important in the talks about India ruling itself.

Gandhi and his wife Kasturbai

40

Gandhi's body was covered in rose petals.

He did his best to calm the fighting between Hindus and **Muslims** when the new country of Pakistan was made in 1947. This made him many enemies.

Some people felt that Pakistan should never have been made. They wanted to fight to get the land back. They knew Gandhi would never agree. They decided they had to get rid of him.

On 30 January 1948, Gandhi was talking to a large crowd in Delhi. He was shot three times. He died at once. More than three million people took part in his funeral procession.

Today, **Mahatma** Gandhi is remembered and respected as a man of peace by people all over the world.

Why was Gandhi called Mahatma?

Gandhi worked in Africa for 20 years. When he returned to India, he was famous.

An Indian poet who had heard about his work in Africa called him "great soul". This was a way of saying how important he felt Gandhi's work had been. The Indian word for great soul is Mahatma. So many people agreed with this description of Gandhi that they began to use it instead of his name. It was a way of showing how much they respected him and how much they admired his work.

Hindus in other countries

This section tells you about Hindus who do not live in India.

There are over 800 million Hindus world-wide. Most of these live in India. After the troubles in 1947, many left India to live in other countries. For example, today there are about 910,000 Hindus in the United States, 360,000 in Britain, and 43,500 in Australia.

Worship in the home

Wherever Hindus live, the most important **worship** takes place in their home.

In countries where most people are not Hindus, children learn about the religion mainly from what they are taught at home.

A Hindu temple in a former church

All Hindu homes have a **shrine**. This may be a separate room, or a shelf in the kitchen or bedroom. Families worship there just as they would in India.

A Hindu temple in Britain

Worship in temples

In India, people do not often worship in a group, except at important temples.

In Britain and other countries where most people are not Hindu, group worship is more important. It means people who share the same religion and background can meet one another.

A Hare Krishna procession in London

Hindus have started to worship together, usually on a Sunday. This is because this fits into the way of life of the country.

Gurus

Hindus do not try to encourage people to **convert** to Hinduism. They believe that each person should find out the truth for themselves, and follow it.

However, many people in other countries have been impressed by Hindu teachings. Hindu teachers are often called **Gurus**. Sometimes they are known as a **swami.**

Hindu groups

Some Gurus have groups of followers who try to carry out the teachings of the Guru in their lives. Many Hindus believe that **meditating** on the teachings of a Guru will help them to avoid being reborn again.

A well-known modern Guru is Swami Prabhupada, who began the group called International Society for Krishna Consciousness in 1967. This group is often called Hare Krishna, because its followers meditate on the name of Krishna.

Other modern Gurus are Sai Baba and Swami Narayan, who work mainly with young Hindus. They encourage them to learn more about Hinduism, and be proud of their background.

Special occasions in childhood

This section tells you about important things that happen to young Hindus.

Samskars
The special ceremonies in a Hindu's life are called **samskars**. Altogether there are 16 samskars. The way to perform them is written in the **holy** books.

Birth
The first three samskars happen before a child is even born. They are prayers asking God to protect the mother and baby. When the baby is born, the time and place of birth are recorded. This is for the baby's horoscope. The baby is washed, then the father places a few drops of honey and ghee in its mouth and says a prayer. This is the fourth samskar.

The naming ceremony
A Hindu baby is usually given its name when it is 12 days old. Hindus believe that choosing the right name is very important. A **priest** is sometimes asked to suggest a letter or sound from which the name is taken.

Friends and relations come to the baby's house. The baby is dressed in new clothes, and placed in a cradle. The eldest woman in the family says what the baby's name is going to be. The father whispers in its ear "Now your name is...". There are songs, and everyone eats a sweet made of fruit, nuts, and sugar. This is the fifth samskar.

As the child grows up, there are three more samskars. The most important is the eighth samskar, which is the child's first haircut.

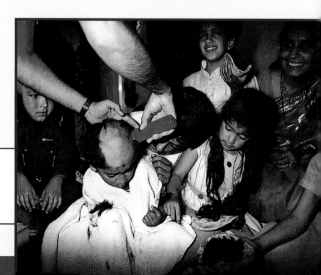

Shaving a boy's head for the eighth samskar

This usually happens when the baby is just over a year old. A boy has his head shaved. It is a way of showing that any bad actions from the life he lived before have been taken away.

The thread ceremony

This is the 10th samskar. It is the time when a boy joins the religion. He is usually aged between 7 and 12. He prepares for the ceremony with the help of a **Guru**.

A loop of cotton is hung over the boy's left shoulder, and hangs down to his right hip.

After this, a boy is counted as a man. He wears the thread all the time for the rest of his life, changing it at **festivals**.

A father giving his son the special thread

Horoscopes

Hindus always take careful note of the exact time and the place that a baby was born. This information is needed to write a horoscope for the baby.

A horoscope is a way of telling the future, based on the position of the stars. Horoscopes for Hindus are written by a priest. He uses information about the baby's parents and the stars to tell what the baby's future will be.

Many Hindus use horoscopes to work out the best time for events, such as weddings, to take place.

Weddings

This section tells you about Hindu weddings.

Hindus think that marriage is important, so that there can be children to carry on the family. Parents usually help their children choose a suitable person to marry. This is called an **arranged marriage.**

In the past, couples did not meet until their wedding day, but today things are not usually so strict. The young people may suggest someone suitable, or at least have met a few times before the wedding.

A Hindu bride

The wedding

A Hindu marriage ceremony lasts about an hour, but the celebrations may last for several days.

The couple sit next to each other in front of a special fire. Their hands are tied together, and water is sprinkled on them. The bride's father "gives" the bride to the bridegroom.

The most important part of the marriage is when the couple take seven steps together.

At each step, they stop and make promises to each other. They are joined by a piece of cloth. One end is hung loosely round the bridegroom's neck.

The couple's hands are tied together.

A Hindu wedding

The other is tied
to the bride's **sari**.
This shows that they
are being joined as
husband and wife.
There are more
prayers and readings.
People throw flower
petals before they
give the couple
wedding presents.
Then everyone shares a meal.

Divorce

The law in India allows divorce, but strict Hindus think marriage
should only be ended when the husband or wife dies.

A Hindu bride

It takes several hours to prepare a Hindu bride for her wedding. She
must look beautiful! The night before her wedding, her hands and
feet are painted in beautiful patterns using a special dye made from
plants. She wears special eye make-up.

Hindu brides wear a new red and gold sari. A sari is what women
usually wear in India. It is a long piece of cloth which is wrapped
around the body so that it becomes a dress. She wears lots of gold
jewellery, especially rings and bracelets. The bride and bridegroom
both wear a garland of flowers like a long necklace.

Funerals

This section tells you about what happens when a Hindu dies.

Hindus believe in rebirth, so they do not think that death is the end. Of course, people are sad, because the person is no longer with them, but funerals are a time for looking forward, too. It is the custom for Hindu funerals to take place on the day after death.

Hindu funerals

When someone dies, their body is washed and placed in a special cloth. The body has flowers put on it, then it is carried on a special stretcher to be **cremated**. If possible, bodies are cremated by one of the **holy** rivers in India. The body is placed on a special fire made of wood. This is called a **funeral pyre**. The eldest son or, if there is no son, another close relative, walks around the funeral pyre carrying a lighted torch. He uses this to set fire to the wood.

There are special prayers and readings from the holy books reminding the people that everyone who dies will be reborn.

It is the duty of the eldest son to remain by the fire until it has gone out. When it has gone out, he collects the ashes.

In Indian cities, and in other countries where bodies cannot be burned in the open air, they are taken to a **crematorium**.

A Hindu funeral

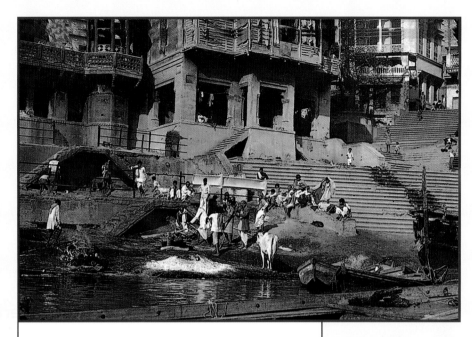

Funeral ghats on the banks of the
River Ganga at Varanasi

The kriya ceremony

The **kriya ceremony** takes place 10 or 12 days after the funeral. Rice and milk are made into offerings. Once this ceremony has been held, Hindus believe that the person's soul has found another body. The family return to their normal life.

Holy rivers

There are seven holy rivers in India. The most holy are the Ganga and the Yamuna. Hindus respect rivers because without water there would be no life, so rivers show that all life on earth comes from God.

Hindus believe that drinking even one drop of water from the Ganga will get rid of everything that you have done wrong in this life and in previous lives. This is why visiting the river and bathing in it are so important for Hindus. They believe that scattering ashes from a funeral on the river will help the person who has died break out of the rebirth cycle.

Glossary

ahimsa idea of non-violence and respect for life

arranged marriage marriage where partners are chosen or suggested by parents

ashrama one of four stages of life for Hindus

atman the soul which is in everything

Aum a sound and sign which Hindus believe is holy. You say the word as if it were written 'Ah-oo-m'

Brahman the ultimate reality, great power

Brahmins first varna (social grouping in Hinduism)

Buddhist follower of the teachings of Buddha

caste another name for a jati

convert become a member of a religion

create make new things

cremate burn a dead body

crematorium place where dead bodies are burned

eternal lasting for ever

fast to go without food and drink for religious reasons

festival time of celebration, for example remembering an event in the life of a god

funeral pyre special "bonfire" to burn a dead body

ghat steps and platform on a river bank

grihastha householder, the second stage of Hindu life

Guru Hindu teacher

Harijans "children of God", untouchables, the lowest group in India's social groupings

holy to do with God

image special statue of a god or goddess in a shrine

incense sweet-smelling spices

jati part of a varna (social grouping in Hinduism)

karma the actions which affect rebirth

kriya ceremony final ceremony after a death

Kshatriyas second varna (social grouping in Hinduism)

Mahatma "great soul", the name given to Gandhi

mandir Hindu temple

meditate emptying your mind so you can think only about God

Muslim follower of Islam

pilgrimage special journey made because of religion

preserve keep things safe

priest man who leads worship

puja general term for Hindu worship of a god or goddess

reincarnation rebirth of the soul

samskar ceremony which marks an important stage in a Hindu's life

Sanatan dharma eternal truths, another term for Hinduism

sannyasin a holy man, the fourth stage of Hindu life

Sanskrit very old language once spoken in India

sari cloth worn as a dress in India

shrine holy place

Shudras fourth varna (social grouping in Hinduism)

sin wrong things that a person has done

soul a person's spirit

swami title given to some Hindu teachers

temple special building for worship

tilak powder placed on the forehead during worship

Vaishyas third varna (social grouping in Hinduism)

varnas four main social groups of people in India

Vedas Hindu holy books

worship show respect and love for a god

Find out more

More books to read

Barnes, Trevor. *World faiths: Hinduism and other eastern religions.* London, Kingfisher, 2005

Nason, Ruth. *Religious lives: Krishna and Hinduism.* London, Hodder Wayland, 2006

Penney, Sue. *World beliefs and cultures: Hinduism.* Oxford, Heinemann Library, 2001

Using the internet

You can find out more about Hinduism in books and on the Internet. Use a search engine such as **www.yahooligans.com** to search for information. A search for the word "Hinduism" will bring back lots of results, but it may be difficult to find the information you want. Try refining your search to look for some of the people and ideas mentioned in this book, such as "Krishna" or "Hindu festivals".

Website

www.bbc.co.uk/religion/religions/hinduism/index
Try looking here for up-to-date information and articles on Hinduism and Hindus.

51

Index

*The numbers in **bold** tell you where you can find out most about the words.*